FROM DAVID~SARA

on my 95th

4

SPIRIT OF

EASTBOURNE

IAIN McGOWAN

First published in Great Britain in 2010

Copyright text and photographs © 2010 Iain McGowan

British Library Cataloguing-in-Publication Data
A CIP record for this title is available from the British Library

ISBN 978 1 906887 33 9

PiXZ Books
Halsgrove House, Ryelands Industrial Estate,
Bagley Road, Wellington, Somerset TA21 9PZ
Tel: 01823 653777
Fax: 01823 216796
email: sales@halsgrove.com

An imprint of Halstar Ltd, part of the Halsgrove group of companies
Information on all Halsgrove titles is available at: www.halsgrove.com

Printed in China by Toppan Leefung Printing Ltd

Introduction

As late as 1813, Eastbourne was simply noted as a small fashionable watering place adjacent to the East Sussex South Downs, consisting mainly of the village of Eastbourne itself over a mile inland and the hamlet of Seahouses overlooking the beach. Southbourne and Meades formed two further isolated communities. In 1851 following the example of Brighton along the coast, the principal landowner the Earl of Burlington – later to become the 7th Duke of Devonshire – started development of the entire area on an ambitious scale. Initially in a conservative Regency manner near the sea, this was shortly followed by distinctly recognisable grand Victorian and Italianate fashions. By the turn of the century red brick and tile hanging from the Weald and decorative gabled frontages had become the more desirable style.

With its wide avenues, elegant villas, pretentious terraces and the often dazzling white opulent hotels or colourful guest houses lining the seafront, the resort has for many years been affectionately known as the 'Empress of the Watering Places'. The 7 km tiered and flower lined promenade, backed by landscaped slopes and gardens at its western extremity adjoining the Downs, extends as far as Langney Point close to the Pevensey Levels. It is this juxtaposition of town planning, local facilities, the aspect of the sea and surrounding countryside and an exceptionally sunny climate that has made Eastbourne such a notable resort, considered by many to be one of the finest in Britain.

Early Eastbourne. A few of the remaining buildings of the hamlet of Seahouses overlooking the beach and now incorporated into the later sea front. (opposite) The view from the pier looking east towards Pevensey. Seahouses is on the left facing Marine Parade.

The twelfth century church of St Mary at the heart of the original village of Eastbourne, an area now known as 'Old Town'.

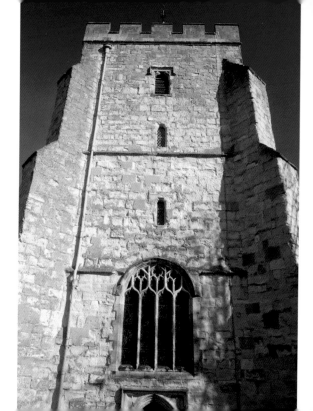

This page and next two pages:
Aspects of Old Town.
Charles Dickens was a regular
visitor to Eastbourne.

Borough House in Borough Lane dating back to the eighteenth century.

Seaside development. The 7th Duke of Devonshire, the man principally
responsible for the foundations of modern Eastbourne.
Opposite: The monumental stuccoed Burlington Hotel, one of the first
major developments to take place, completed in the 1850s.

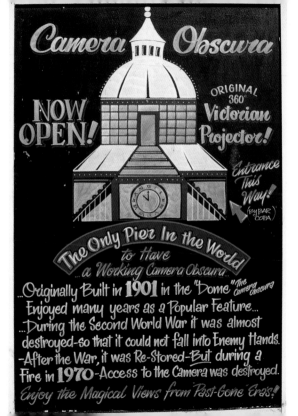

Opposite: Eastbourne's central seafront area looking back from the pier. The 300m pier designed by Eugenius Birch and opened in 1872 is unique in featuring a rare Camera Obscura under one of its domes.

Restored bathing machine in the care of the Langham Hotel, one of only a few surviving machines remaining from the many thousands once to be found on the beaches of the Sussex seaside resorts.

The famous seafront 'carpet gardens' with the pier beyond.

A brass plaque adorns a drinking fountain dated 1865.

Opposite: Eastbourne's pier at dusk.

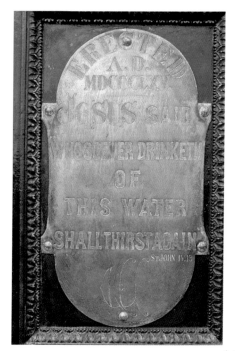

Pages 18–21: Seaside architecture in Regency, Victorian and Grand Italianate styles.

Looking west along the opulent Grand Parade seafront on an early summer's day.

The essential striped chairs of an English seaside resort.

This page and opposite: High summer in Eastbourne.

OPENED BY

THE RT. HON
LORD LECONFIELD
G.C.V.O.
LORD LIEUTENANT
OF SUSSEX
ON THE
5TH AUGUST 1935

COUNCILLOR
MISS THORNTON J.P.
MAYOR

ALDERMAN
Lt.Col. ROLAND GWYNNE
D.S.O., D.L., J.P.
CHAIRMAN OF THE COMMITTEE

LESLIE ROSEVEARE
M.INST. C.E.
BOROUGH ENGINEER

MELIORA SEQUIMUR

This page and opposite:
The Art Deco seafront bandstand
completed in 1935 is one of the
town's most popular attractions.
Featuring varying programmes
almost daily over the summer season
by local or visiting brass and concert
bands and celebrities, the bandstand
is particularly noted for the quality
of its acoustics.

Within the bandstand a plaque honours John Wesley Woodward who played with several of Eastbourne's orchestras and who tragically drowned in April 1912 whilst a member of the ship's orchestra of the ill-fated *Titanic*.

A sea fret rolls in across the beach to soften the outline of the pier on an early summer's morning.

This page and opposite:
Seaside colour at the pier.

This page and opposite:
Reflections on a more genteel age!
The metal plaques on this page can still
be found along Grand Parade near the
Wish Tower. The various letters denote
standing areas such as Hackney
Carriage Stand, Motor Cycle Stand,
Bath Chair Stand etc.

2

THIS CHALET WAS USED BY THEIR MAJESTIES KING GEORGE V
AND QUEEN MARY IN THE MONTH OF MARCH. 1935

The view west along a busy lower promenade towards Holywell with its seafront chalets and the rising chalk cliffs beyond.
Opposite: One of the chalets still proudly displays a reminder of two famous visitors.

An early spring day along the promenade.

The circular brick Redoubt fortress, now a museum, once featured ten cannon overlooking the sea.

Above: Part of the Wish Tower, originally constructed as one of a series of Martello Towers between 1805 - 1810 along the south coast as a defence against a feared Napoleonic invasion.

The eastern extremity of the
promenade and shingle beach
is still used for recreational
sailing activities and sales of
locally caught fish.

Ever popular fishing off the end of the pier.

Away from the seafront, the richly ornate Town Hall constructed in the mid 1880s in Grove Road.

Opposite page:
The church of St Saviour and St Peter, designed by the eminent architect G E Street, principally built in red brick and completed in 1866. The broach spire was added later. The photograph shows part of the Blessed Sacrament Chapel with the nave beyond.

Part of the striking multi-coloured brick station building rebuilt by the London, Brighton and South Coast Railway in 1886.

Following the arrival of the railway in 1849, Terminus Road linking the station with the seafront slowly developed as the town's principal shopping centre and now features a wide range of pubs, cafés, restaurants, shops and larger stores.

The Edwardian atmosphere of Grove Road.

Sculptured figure and window
detail of the central library
dating back to the early 1960s.

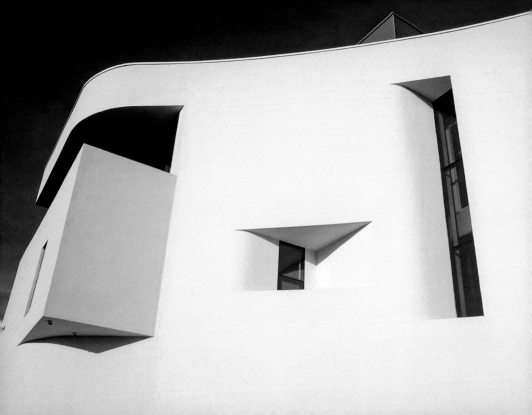

The classical Winter Garden of the 1870s overlooking Devonshire Park.
Opposite: The new Towner Art Gallery designed by Rick Mather Architects and completed in 2009. The gallery sited immediately adjacent to the contemporary Congress Theatre has already been described as one of the leading venues for visual arts in south east England.

Seafront details.

Opposite:
An ethereal sense of
space and colour.

Pages 50–53
Scenes at the recently completed award winning Sovereign Harbour – often referred to as Little Venice and now one of the largest marina complexes in Northern Europe.

Coast and countryside – Beachy Head. Immediately west of Eastbourne as the South Downs meet the white chalk cliffs rise to a height of 163m and with the prominent red and white striped lighthouse below, the Head has become one of the most famous landmarks in England.
Opposite: The dramatic perpendicular Seven Sisters cliffs beyond Beachy Head viewed from near Birling Gap.

Right: The fourteenth century timber-framed Clergy House at Alfriston was the first building to be purchased by the National Trust in 1896 for the grand sum of £10. It is a particularly fine example of a traditional Wealden 'Hall' House from this period.

Below: On the east bank of the River Cuckmere the attractive village of Littlington still features the Littlington Tea Gardens dating back to the nineteenth century and claimed to be the oldest tea gardens in Sussex.

The view from a shoulder of Windover Hill looking towards Folkington,
the outer suburbs of Eastbourne and the distant Pevensey Levels.

The 73m high Long Man of Wilmington cut out of the chalk downland of Windover Hill. His age and purpose are still unknown.
Opposite: The classic view of the East Sussex Downs seen from near Wilmington.

The rough flint and stone church of St Peter at Folkington dating back to 1250 and situated on the very outskirts of Eastbourne.

Left: Part of the broad Anglo-Saxon tower of the church of St Andrew at Jevington.

Below: The fourteenth century church at Lullington at the foot of the Downs, often described as one of England's smallest churches, is simply all that remains of a once larger medieval structure.

Rustic decoration to the Horse and Groom Inn at Polegate.
Opposite: The nineteenth century brick tower Polegate windmill complete with
original machinery restored in 1967 and now open to visitors.

Roman walling, Pevensey Castle. A castle was built here in about 1100 shortly
after the Norman invasion and within the walls of the third century Roman Fort
of Anderida. Described as the finest Roman monument in the county, it was
within these walls that William the Conqueror and his army spent their first
night on English soil prior to the fateful battle of 1066.